COTSWOLD DRIV

THE SOUTHERN COTSWOLDS

written and illustrated

by

Peter T. Reardon

DRIVEABOUT SERIES ®

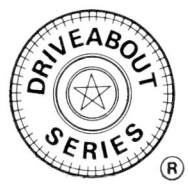

Published by

REARDON & SON
CHELTENHAM, ENGLAND

Copyright © 1978
Reardon & Son

Cotswold Driveabout
the Southern Cotswolds

5th Edition 1990

ISBN 0 9508674 2 X

Printed by
Hayman & Son (Printers) Ltd.,
Bennington Street, Cheltenham.

THE COTSWOLDS

The Cotswolds, with their beauty supreme,
A rambler's pleasure, an artist's dream.
Within these undulating hills abound
Enjoyment for all, in sight and sound.

Tall trees give a proud and noble scene,
Whilst the fields show a calm and placid green.
The dawns and sunsets give colourful thrills
When viewed from the tops of these glorious hills.

Ancient buildings and monuments are to be found
In towns whose names have a very quaint sound,
And streams and rivers wend their musical way
Past banks, with wild flowers, both colourful and gay.

In winter, the hills appear harsh and foreboding
In their white coats of snow and caps of grey clouding,
From the strong, icy winds, there is little respite
Howling and whistling by day and by night.

Cotswold beauty survives winter without coming to harm
And returns in the new spring with added charm.

ALFRED KING

INTRODUCTION

The Cotswolds

The Cotswolds — intriguing, majestic, even cruel in its own way. There is a bigness that is breathtaking, especially during the summer, a loneliness that can be frightening during the winter, but always a grandeur, as powerful as an exciting tale that not one little bit must be missed. Perhaps early man found the excitement of these hills a good reason for settling in them. They offered a natural fortification in many instances for settlements, often with views over the valley of the Severn, where animals could be hunted and fish caught in the river. There were also numerous small rivers which offered fish, water and game.

Today, we still go up into these hills, but for a different reason. We go to see the places where these people lived and buried their dead, to marvel at the views, stand where they stood some 5,000 years ago. The excitement is still there. The vision can be captured by the canvas or the camera and the blood can be stirred by the pen of the writer. The urge to return is strong.

The Romans came, stayed a while and then left. They were about the first to leave us monuments of their advanced way of life that we can understand today. Then came the Saxons, the Danes and the Normans. Each left something by which to remember them. In more recent times great houses have been built and are there for all to see, each giving something to history and in particular, the Cotswolds. Some of these features have been included in this little book, so that you can be acquainted in words and pictures, with but a few of the details that make up the wonderful story of these hills.

It is hoped that your visit to the Cotswolds will be most enjoyable, and if, with the help of these pages, more memorable, then the object of this publication will have been achieved.

Do come again.

Peter T. Reardon

Leckhampton,
Cheltenham Spa.
1978.

Cheltenham Spa

An excellent centre from which to tour the Cotswolds and a beautiful town in itself. A Regency style Spa with fine hotels, shopping centre second to none, lovely parks and gardens, all set in elegant tree-lined roads at the foot of the Cotswold Hills overlooking the Severn Valley and Welsh mountains. Cheltenham is famous for its Spa Waters, discovered in 1718 by, not a man, but pigeons. Hence the pigeons in the Town's coat of Arms. After George III's visit to the town in 1788, it became the fashionable thing to come to Cheltenham Spa and partake of the mineral waters. The waters are still available at the Pittville Pump Rooms and Town Hall should visitors wish to sample them. It is an interesting fact that these springs produce the only natural alkaline Spa Water in the country fit for human consumption. The little drawing on the right above shows one of the urns found in the Town Hall from which the Waters may be drawn. The entertainment calendar is very full and specific details can be obtained from the Tourist Information Centre.

Painswick

A small Cotswold town, famous most, perhaps, for its churchyard with 99 yew trees. It is said that the 100th will not grow, but if it does another dies soon. Some are as much as 200 years old. The walls of this 15th century church still bears traces of flames that were intended to burn out refugees during the Civil War. The lychgate shown on the right is at the west corner of the churchyard. Timbers from the old belfry were used in its construction, and interesting carved bargeboards can be seen. Behind the south-east churchyard wall are the 'spectacle stocks', unique, inasmuch as they are believed to be the only ones in existence in the country. For those exploring Painswick on foot, there is much to see in the town. Though not spectacular, it makes one feel quite detached from the rush of modern living. The Little Fleece Bookshop in Bisley Street is a fine example of a Cotswold town house. Painswick lies on the A46(T) Stroud to Cheltenham road, about 4 miles north of Stroud.

Stroud

An important centre since the middle of the 14th century for the weaving of cloth, once made from the fleeces of Cotswold sheep, Stroud still has a number of mills working today. Along the banks of the River Frome

numerous factories and works will be found, many having connections with the cloth industry in some way. Famous for its good quality the material has a world-wide demand. Industry is still expanding in and around the town today, but many are of modern variety. Stroud also has its lighter side when work is done as can be seen pictured on the right of this unusual inn sign spanning Union Street. It is unusual in that inn signs actually extending across streets like this could probably be counted on the fingers of one hand. The town lies at the intersection of the A46(T) Cheltenham to Bath road with the A419 Gloucester to Cirencester road.

Rodborough

At the most northernmost tip of Rodborough Common, 600ft above sea level stands Rodborough Fort pictured here below. Impressive as it is to look at, it is not unfortunately, a genuine medieval fort, being built in the last century. Rodborough Common, like the adjoining Minchinhampton Common, is almost exclusively National Trust Property, and lies in the southern confluence of the A46(T) and A419 at Stroud. Exciting views over the Stroud and Nailsworth Valleys are possible on fine days from both Commons. Walks, kite flying and picnics can be enjoyed and there is plenty of room for parking.

Nailsworth

Reclining in a valley about 4 miles south of Stroud, Nailsworth has its associations with the wool trade of the Cotswolds. On the right is a sketch of a memorial to William Smith, a lawyer. It also served as a drinking fountain, but in recent years was moved on account of a road reconstruction plan and is not now connected to a water supply. Behind this memorial is Day's Mill, once used for weaving cloth in the 18th century. After turning left at the Clock Tower, the first turn right goes up to Minchinhampton via the Devil's Elbow, and the second turn right is the way to the Common by way of either Nailsworth Ladder, or the Double U, (both old pack-horse trails

and later used as Motor Club trials hills), and the village of Watledge. Nailsworth straddles the junction of the A46 Cheltenham to Bath road and the B4014 Malmesbury/Tetbury to Nailsworth road.

Berkeley Castle (H.H.A.)

In the Vale of Berkeley, part of the Severn Valley, lies Berkeley Castle, formidable and awe inspiring. Its history is closely linked with the Cotswolds and for this reason it is felt that it should be included in this little book. The Castle has been occupied by the Berkeley family right through from when it was built in the 12th century to the present time. At the time of the Civil War, 1642-9, much damage was done to the Castle, including breaching the west wall of the keep. The gatehouse shown on tne right is at the car park entrance on the B4066. Edward Jenner, best known for his discovery of vaccination came from the town of Berkeley. For a short time he lived in Cheltenham, but returned to Berkeley in later years where he died. Just a few paces from the Castle entrance can be seen the famed Jenner museum and his cottage, and the little building like a 'retreat' which he used as a surgery for treatment. His tomb is in the church just across the way.

Christ Church, in an Alpine Setting at Chalford

Chalford

Known as the Alpine Village of the Cotswolds, Chalford lies on the northern slopes of the Golden Valley overlooking the River Frome. The previous page shows Christ Church from high ground with the other side of the

Golden Valley looking towards Minchinhampton. The old Severn and Thames Canal flowed through this valley from Framilode on the Severn, to join the Thames at Lechlade via a $2\frac{1}{4}$ mile long tunnel at Daneway, Sapperton. The picture above is of natural springs known as the Tankard Springs, and have never been known to run dry. They can be found in the High Street not very far from Christ Church. Opposite the church is a Round House once used by lengthsmen on the canal, but is now a small museum. Close by is a pair of very old gear wheels from Sevilles Mill sluice gates, now mounted on a stone base, presented by the partners of Elbesee Products in 1970, European Conservation Year. Nearby is a culvert with a milestone over it reading Walsbridge 4, Inglesham $24\frac{3}{4}$. Chalford is on the A419, 4 miles from Stroud and 8 miles west of Cirencester.

Nags Head

This little hamlet lies a mile east of Avening on an unclassified road to Cherrington. The drawing shows a decorated panel on the front of the old inn. Not all decoration, it does serve a useful purpose, that of bee hives, access to them being from an upstairs room. A short distance away to the north is Aston Down airfield when, during right conditions, gliding can be watched. 3 miles north west is Minchinhampton, an old wool town with its Market House of 1698, a fine example of this kind of building. Holy Trinity Church has interest outside and in its contents, there being memorials to many local gentry.

Hetty Pegler's Tump

Half way between Dursley and Cainscross just off the B4066 is the village of Nympsfield. Nearly a mile north west of the village is the Nympsfield Long Barrow, twice excavated, the second time just before World War II. It is now, fortunately, in the care of the Dept. of the Environment. 400yds. to the south of Nympsfield Long Barrow is Coaley Peak. From here wonderful views can be obtained, with information of what, where and how far away can be found on an octagonal topograph very conveniently sited on the Peak. Car parking, picnic area and nature walks are available so there is lots of fun for all the family. A mile south of Nympsfield Long Barrow is Hetty Pegler's Tump, a burial mound and chambers  in good condition. Two of the five chambers have been sealed off because they were considered unsafe. The plan of both barrows is similar. On the right above is a little drawing showing the entrance to Hetty Pegler's Tump. Half a mile south again is Uleybury hill fort, an iron-age camp site some 2 - 3000 years old covering almost 40 acres, the best in the country.

North Nibley

Best known for the Tyndale Monument on Nibley Knoll, there is virtually nothing for the fun seeking visitor at North Nibley. If one's pleasures involve rambles, scenery and history then there is much enjoyment to be gained around Nibley. The little drawing on the right shows the Tyndale Monument, viewed from the B4060 Dursley to Wotton-under-Edge road. Erected in 1866 in memory of William Tyndale, the English writer who, in 1525, produced his translation of the New Testament. He was burnt at the stake in Antwerp, Belgium, in 1536 for being a heretic. It was built here because it is believed he was born at North Nibley. Standing 650ft. above sea level overlooking the Severn Valley and Welsh Mountains to the west, the structure is 100ft. high with a flight of steps leading to the top where breathtaking views may be enjoyed on a clear day. From the M5 Motorway, the Monument can be seen for about 13 or 14 miles from north of junction 15 to half way to Gloucester.

Dursley

Nestling on the slopes of a promontory of the western Cotswold escarpment, Dursley is perhaps a suitable place from which to start for some very pleasant walks and rambles. Although now much industrialised, the town is still very quaint with its old buildings flanking steep winding little streets. The Church of St. James dates from about the 15th century, and the Market House, opposite was built in 1738. A statue of Queen Anne, high up on the east wall of the Market House is shown in the sketch on the right. Dursley lies on the A4135 Tetbury to the A38 road, about 4 miles from Cambridge (Glos) and 13 miles from Tetbury.

Kingswood

A little town just over a mile south of Wotton-under-Edge on the B4060. At one time a place of some importance, a great Cistercian Abbey having been built here by the Normans. At the Dissolution in Henry VIII's time most of it was pulled down leaving only the lady chapel as a church for local people. In the early 1700's this was subsequently cannibalised to provide material for a new church that was to be built.

The picture on the right shows the abbey gate house, all that is left of this great house of God. For opening times contact your local Tourist Information Centre.

Duntisbourne Rouse

A very small village nestling on the hillside overlooking the River Dun. The main feature of the village is perhaps the little Church of St Michael, with Saxon as well as Norman work. The location of the church, on such a steep bank as it is, made easy the building of a crypt beneath the chancel. In itself not unusual, even in small Cotswold churches, but to have a footpath and doorway at crypt-floor level is almost unique. In a recess just by this door is a stairway that led to the Chancel but is now sealed up. From the picture of the Church from the churchyard, the slope of the ground can be seen. The doorway to the crypt is not visible because a large tomb is in the way. Once through the lych gate and along the grass walk, access to the churchyard is through a slatted wooden gate. There is an interesting scissor-type iron gate right alongside, allowing one person at a time to go through. Duntisbourne Rouse is only a mile north of Daglingworth, described below.

Daglingworth

A small village 3 miles north of Cirencester just to the west of Ermine Way, the A417(T). The Church of The Holy Rood will of course, provide much of the interest for the visitor to Daglingworth. There is much that is old, with examples of Roman, Saxon and Norman work. Over the doorway to the porch is a sundial of Saxon origin, one of the finest in the country. The drawing on the next page is of the church viewed from the west. Near the church, there is, as shown in the little sketch below, a circular type of dove cote with a revolving ladder inside to enable the 500 nesting boxes round the wall to be reached. Today Daglingworth is part of the Duchy of Cornwall after its adoption, in 1970, by H.R.H. The Prince of Wales.

THE DELIGHTFUL LITTLE CHURCH at DAGLINGWORTH, in GLOUCESTERSHIRE

Wotton-under-Edge

One of the little old market towns that owes its share to the wool trade of the 15th to 16th century, Wotton has some very fine old buildings with something that will interest even the casual visitor. The present-day Wotton Manor was built on the foundations of an earlier house which was sacked by Lord Berkeley's men in 1469, after about 30 years of intermittent feuding and bloodshed. On the corner of Market Street is the old Tolsey, with its very ornate clock, shown in the sketch above, protruding into the High Street. Above the clock face is a portrait of Queen Victoria flanked by the dates of succession to the throne in 1837 and Diamond Jubilee in 1897. The old Grammar School is one of the oldest seats of learning in the country, one of its scholars being Edward Jenner, famous for his discovery of vaccination. The Church of St. Mary has its features and is certainly worth a visit. Wotton-under-Edge lies on the B4058 Bristol to Nailsworth road at the junction with the B4060 Chipping Sodbury to Cam road.

Cricklade

A little old town with a lot of history behind it straddling the Ermin Way, or A419(T) as we know it today, about 7 miles SE of Cirencester. Cricklade, lying in a large area of flat agricultural land just over the border into Wiltshire, is the first town on the River Thames. History has involved the town since the days of the Romans, and in the cemetery can be seen a part of a wall, believed to be a fragment from Saxon times when there was a wall and ditch form of defence. The Severn and Thames Canal passed half a mile away at the north end of town but is now unfortunately derelict. The little drawing on the right shows the town clock at the junction of the B4041 and B4040, just off the A419(T). It is a well known landmark to travellers of the old Cirencester to Swindon road.

South Cerney

At one time maybe better known for the airfield and RAF Station, South Cerney is fast becoming the "Water Sport Metropolis" of the Cotswolds. The Cotswold Marina, to give it its correct name, has a wide variety of facilities laid on, even to giving sailing or water ski instruction. Situated just off the A419, the old Ermine Way, about 4 miles south of Cirencester, it is quite close to South Cerney. The village boasts a recorded history going back over 1000 years. The Church of All Hallows goes back to Norman times or earlier, but was altered considerably in the last century. Much of the old was incorporated with the new. At one time a farming community, South Cerney has undergone several changes in its local occupations, the Cotswold Marina being the latest.

The picture above shows what is now a small folly, but may have previously been a windmill for corn grinding in the height of the farming era, between South Cerney and Siddington.

Thames Head

"Old Father Thames keeps rolling along, down to the mighty sea". So goes the song. But where from? The official source is at Thames Head, near Kemble, just north of the old Fosse Way (A433) at Thames Head Bridge. A rock-strewn pool indicates the spring from which the Thames or Isis is presumed to flow. The illustration shows Neptune at this source at Thames Head. He did, unfortunately, suffer damage by vandals and now reclines in a position overlooking St. John's Lock at Lechlade. St. John's Lock and Bridge lies about a mile east of Lechlade on the A417 Lechlade to Faringdon road. The generally accepted source of the Thames is at Seven Springs, about 4 miles south of Cheltenham, at the junction of the A435 Cheltenham to Cirencester road with the A436 Air Balloon Inn to Stow-on-the-Wold road. These springs do not dry up, as at Thames Head, and form the head of the River Churn, the farthest point of the Thames tributaries from London bridge.

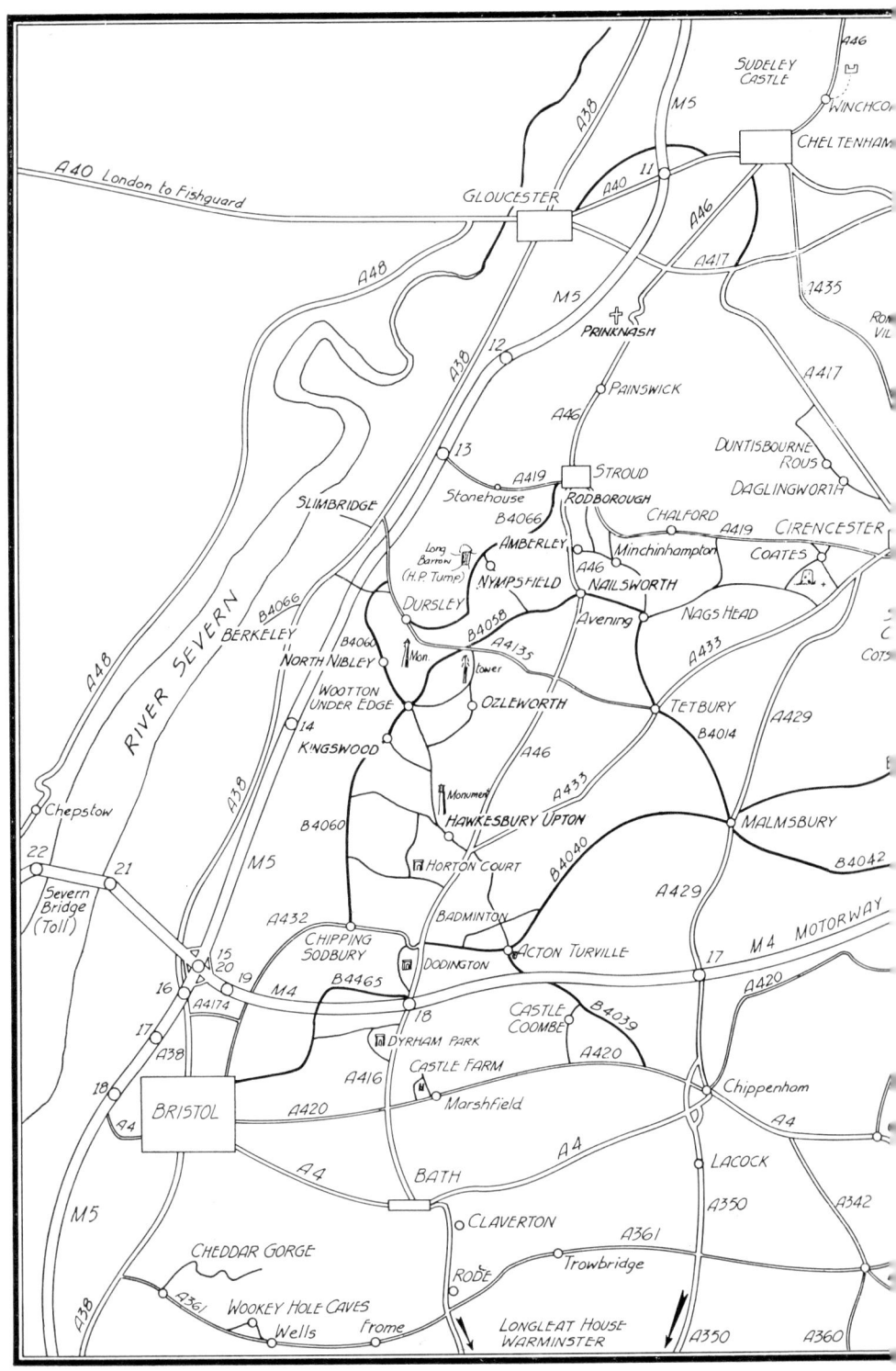

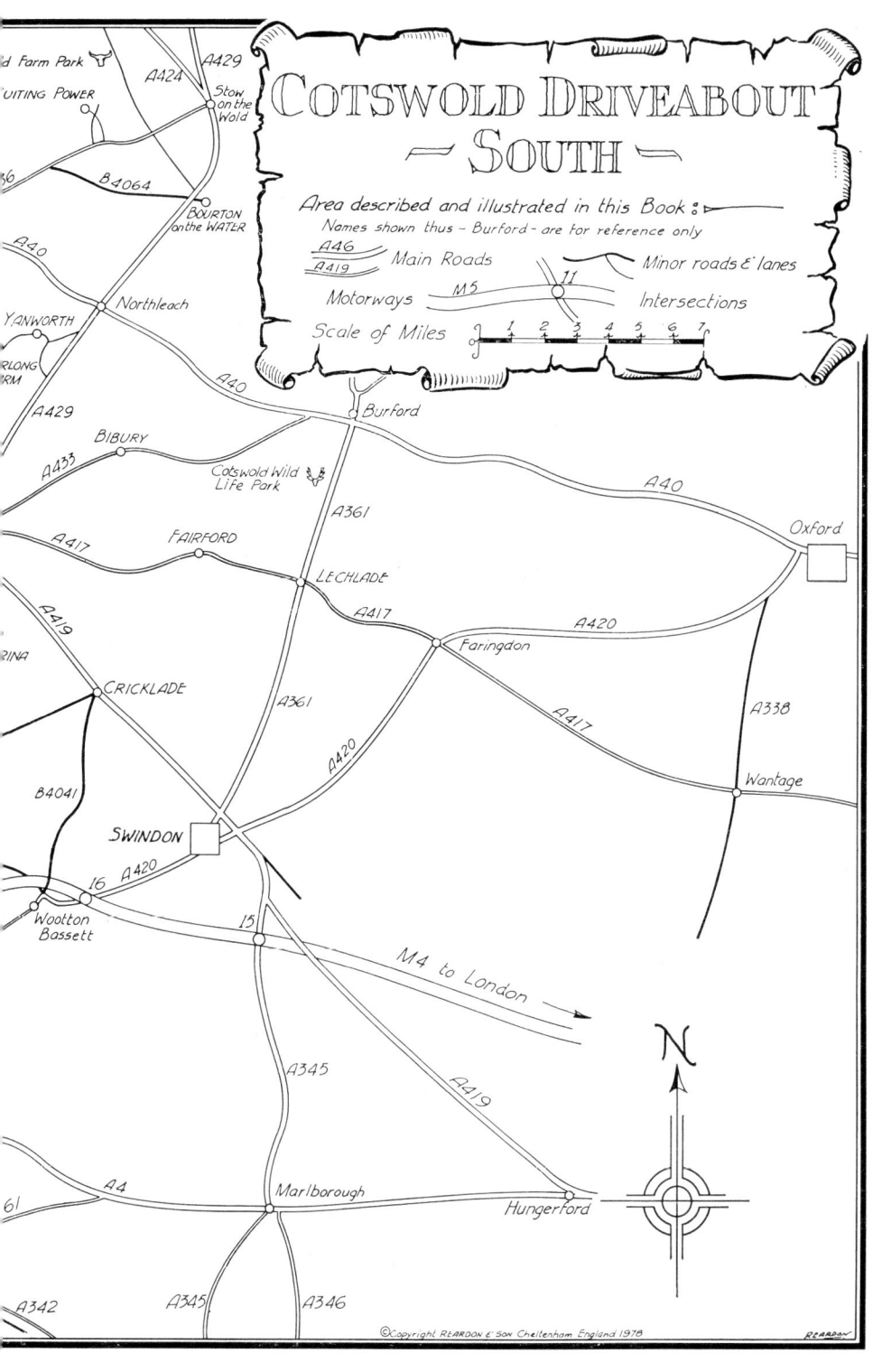

Amberley

Set on the western slopes of Minchinhampton Common at about 550ft., Amberley overlooks the Nailsworth Valley towards Woodchester Park on the other side. Just a small gathering of various buildings, among them Rose Cottage. Mrs. Craik, who wrote the novel "John Halifax, Gentleman", lived here and much of the story included Amberley and Rose Cottage under different names of course. "Abel Fletcher's Mill" at Tewkesbury, some twenty miles north (as the crow flies) on the A38 was also the scene of many doings in the tale. The little drawing on the right shows a monument erected to commemorate Queen Victoria's reign in June, 1897. It can be seen at the cross roads in the village opposite the Inn. Up on the common above Amberley there is plenty of room for  ball games with the family or just plain walking. For those interested in archaeology there are a number of features to be seen some dating back nearly 3,000 years. A little way from here, SE of Minchinhampton, is Gatcombe Park, the home of Princess Anne.

Fairford

Fairford is a picturesque town — truly Cotswold. The Old Mill pictured on the opposite page must be a familiar sight to many of our American allies who were stationed here during the '39-'45 War. Famous for its 28 painted windows is the 15th century Church of St. Mary, shown in the distance across the field and River Coln. The Mill is now a private residence. John Keble, who was educated at Corpus Christi College, Oxford, and became professor of poetry at 39, was born in Fairford in 1792. Keble College, Oxford, was built in his memory in 1870. The Town is well provided with inns. Pictured right is the best of the Cotswold tiler's craft with its variations in direction and angle of slope. This example shows the back of The Bull as seen from the A417.

THE OLD MILL, FAIRFORD.

Cirencester

A town that has figured in the history of the country, county and Cotswolds since it was just a settlement of the Boduni tribe. When the Romans invaded Britain for the second time, they marched over the Cotswolds to a spot  where they came across this settlement, and it was here that they built a fortress which was to become the foundation of the town of Corinium. (the town we know as Cirencester). When the Romans left Britain in 410 A.D., Cirencester was an important administration centre and a very well planned town, but it did not take the local English people long to plunder the town, leaving nature to do the rest. When eventually a new town began to rise, it did not follow the Roman pattern, so absolute was the destruction. Today there is an excellent museum in Park Street, showing relics of Roman times some of which have been dug up as a result of road and building works in more recent years. The picture above shows the remains of the Hospital and Chantry of St. John the Evangelist, in Spitalgate Lane, which was founded by Henry II in the 12th century. So, too, was a great abbey only to be destroyed some 400 years later at the Dissolution of the Monastries in 1539. All that is left now is what is known as the Spital Gate (from Hospital Gate) shown on the page opposite with a fine Norman style archway. This gateway was probably built by the early English learning much of the art of building from the Normans. Of much later date is the Barracks at Cecily Hill, in a quiet niche away from much of the towns bustle near the very imposing gates of Cirencester Park. The Park is open for visitors to the town to enjoy walks and picnics, but motor vehicles are not allowed. One of the features to be found in the Park is a little structure called Pope's Seat, a kind of summer house where the poet, Alexander Pope, used to be a frequent visitor. Cirencester is siutated at the intersection of the Fosse Way and Ermin Street, or the A433 and A417(T) as we know it today.

The Round House, Coates

In the early 1800's the Severn & Thames Canal was operating to carry bulk goods from Bristol to London. To help pay for the upkeep of the canal, tolls had to be collected. This was done by dividing the canal up into sections and tollkeepers living in round houses similar to the one shown in the sketch, could collect their dues from the boats as they went from section to section. To prevent boats slipping past without paying, a stout chain was drawn across the canal at these points just under the water line. The remains of the round house shown can be found about a mile SW of the village of Coates on the south bank of the canal. Much work has been done on this part of the canal including restoring the south portal of the tunnel. Coates lies about 4 miles west of Cirencester just south of the A419, Cirencester to Stroud road.

Malmesbury

Old, in fact very old, is this town of Malmesbury, dating back to about the 5th century. Its religious origins evolved around the late 600's, culminating in a beautiful abbey being built during the Norman period. The door and porch can be seen on the south side, and has some of the finest carving perhaps in the world today, there being about 75 pictures from the scriptures carved on a series of stone bands running right round the door. Fortunately, the entire structure was not razed at the Dissolution, the nave and porch being left standing and serving as the church to this day. Near the junction of the A429 and A434 stands the 15th century Market Cross, shown in the picture on the right. Described as expensive at the time of building it was also useful for holding market on wet days.

Tetbury

A small town with a history going back to Saxon times. It owes most of its fine buildings to the great wool trade of the 15th and 16th centuries. The centre of the town is marked by the famous old Market House standing on twenty-one pillars.

Built in 1650, it was restored and altered in the early 1800's to much as it is today. The weathervane is interesting, being a pair of dolphins. Sheep might have been more in keeping with the times one would think. Not too big to walk round, there is much that can be seen of interest to those liking old buildings and architectural details. With the Market House at the centre of the town, Tetbury lies at the junction of the A433 from Cirencester and the B4014, Nailsworth to Malmesbury road.

GPO Tower near Ozleworth

You would be wrong if you thought this structure in the drawing here was an observation platform for visitors to view the Cotswolds. It is in fact one of a network of GPO Radio Towers. This particular one is a micro-wave Relay Station, linking telephone calls from Plymouth, Cardiff and Bristol with the famous GPO Radio Tower in London. With the aid of these towers and satelites like Telstar, phone calls can be made to most parts of the world through international telephone linkups. This modern erection, built of reconstructed stone and standing 240ft. high, can be found 2 miles south of the junction of the A4135 Dursley to Tetbury road and B4058 Wotton-under-Edge to Nailsworth road, in a glorious spot over 750ft. above sea level overlooking Ozleworth Park in the south and Tyley Bottom and Wotton-under-Edge in the west.

Castle Combe

One of the lovely and unspoilt villages of England, Castle Combe nestles in the wooded valley through which flows the little By Brook. In the 1960's, people with all kinds of equipment invaded the village to make film sequences for the movie "Dr. Doolittle", and the cottages, bridge and stream at the southern end of the village became a fishing harbour overnight. Not surprising really that Castle Combe was selected for this role as it was once claimed to be the prettiest village in all England. About a mile to the east on the B4039 is the Motor Racing Circuit which has made Castle Combe famous in the sporting world. The circuit, of approx. 2 miles, stages six or seven National Championship Events during the year. The little drawing on the right above shows the old stone Market Cross with the pump still by its side, unfortunately not now in working order, and with what is known as the Butter Cross just on the left of it. On page 24 opposite, the drawing shows the approach to Castle Combe down through the trees after leaving the B4039 Acton Turville to Yatton Keynell road.

Hawkesbury Upton

On the right is a drawing of the Somerset Monument standing some 650ft. above sea level overlooking the village of Hawkesbury Upton. About 120ft. high, there are 144 steps to reach the platform at the top. It was erected in memory of General Lord Robert Somerset, the fourth son of Henry, 5th Duke of Beaufort. His remains were interred in St. Peter's Church in Hanover Square. The monument was designed by Lewis Vulliamy and built in 1846. Lewis was born in Pall Mall in 1791, exhibited many designs at the Royal Academy during his life and died in 1871. The Church of St. Mary in Hawkesbury has much to interest the visitor here both inside and out. Mostly 15th century, there are some earlier remnants. At the road junction in Hawkesbury Upton is an old pump and cross, the pump being used up to the war time when mains water was laid on.

Westonbirt Arboretum (Forestry Commission)
About 3 miles south-west of Tetbury on the west side of the A433 lies Westonbirt Arboretum. Here, amid wonderful trees and shrubs, an exciting day can be enjoyed by all, and appreciated by those who have little interest in trees and forestry. Trees from all parts of the world can be found here and, depending upon the season, an abundance of colour is always to be seen. Perhaps the most spectacular time is during the Autumn, when deciduous trees are changing colour and making what appears to be a patchwork carpet of reds and golds on a green base. The Arboretum covers 161 acres and there is ample car parking, with facilities for refreshments, souvenirs, library and inform-

ation. Once privately owned, it is now in the care of the Forestry Commission whose acquisition in 1956 will ensure continuance of the fine work that was started in 1829. Pictured above right is the memorial to Sir Robert Holford, whose vision and foresight spurred him on to undertake this mammoth project.

Chipping Sodbury
Almost at the southernmost part of the Cotswolds lies the "Sodburys". They are a group of three, Chipping, Old and Little. Just after World War II, Chipping and Old Sodbury were formed into one Parish and today, they are, geographically, one town. The history of the Sodburys goes back to before Roman times and many interesting discoveries have been made. In the picture on the right below is shown a clock tower above a building. The clock was originally a memorial to Lt. Col. George William Blathwayt of Dyrham Park, some four miles south of Chipping Sodbury. In later years an addition in the form of public conveniences was made around it, and then finally a concrete shelter with seats was added in more recent times. It now also serves as the local bus stop. The Sodburys lie on the A432 near the junction with the A46 Bath to Stroud to Cheltenham road, about 3 miles north of junction 18 of the M4 Motorway.

Acton Turville

A quaint little village at the junction of the B4039 and B4040 with a railway station only 200 yards away. Just over a mile to the north is Badminton Park. Built in the latter half of the 17th century, Badminton has been the family seat of the Dukes of Beaufort ever since. The scene of the famous Badminton Three Day Event Horse Trials. The stables and kennels have limited opening times for those wishing to see them, as with the House itself. There is interesting furniture and fine artworks by English, Dutch and Italian painters. On the south-east corner of the Park is a long barrow called the Giant's Cave. It has been excavated twice, once by an Edinburgh team who took all the remains back to their museum. It was, unfortunately, damaged during road reconstruction. Three big stones remain in the centre and it seems possible that there was a dry-stone wall surrounding the tomb. Being a very tall race of people they would of course, have looked like giants to the smaller, more common tribes. On the right above is a picture of the Well at Acton Turville, and it will be seen that the portcullis emblem is also found in the Coat of Arms of the Dukes of Beaufort.

Dodington House

In beautiful surroundings, landscaped by Capability Brown in the late 1760's, the present house was built at the end of the 18th Century for Christopher B. Codrington. Up until just a few years ago, Dodington House was open to the public. The House, Grounds and Exhibitions made it one of the major attractions in the Southern Cotswolds, and we hope that in the near future it will once again open its doors. The sketch on the right shows the bust of a girl covering a well which once fed a pool that was used for bathing. Lying on the west side of the A46(T) Bath to Stroud road about 200 yards north of junction 18 on the M4 Motorway. Dodington Park is quite easy to find.

Dyrham Park (National Trust)

One of the historic houses of England built in a cleft of the western escarpment of the Cotswolds at a height of 450ft. above sea level. The views to the west and over Bristol are wonderful. To the north, east and south the parklands rise to nearly 600ft. Landscaped by Capability Brown and later by Humphrey Repton in the early 1800's, the park remains much the same as at that time. Over the turn from the 17th to 18th century the house was rebuilt and enlarged that very little remains of the old place. Today, Dyrham Park has much to offer the visitor. The house, attractive in itself, holds many interesting treasures of furniture, pictures, tapestries, china etc. There is over 200 acres of Deer Park open for walks and picnics. The little Church of St. Peter, right beside the house has its share of interest. The sketch above shows Neptune in his 18th century position, which is all that remains of a 224 step water cascade down to a pool in front of the house. The house and grounds are now in the care of the National Trust. Dyrham Park is located about 2 miles south of the M4 Motorway junction 18 on the A46(T) Cheltenham/Stroud to Bath road.

Castle Farm

A small private Folk Museum to interest anyone who loves the countryside. At the time of updating this book we were unable to ascertain its opening times, so we suggest contacting a local Tourist Information Centre before making a visit. The oldest building of the group dates from about 1550-1600 and is the original farmhouse or Long House. It is a two-storey abode of cruck construction. This building housed the farmer and his family at one end with the animals in the other half, while above was sleeping space and animal fodder. The picture shows the fireplace in the Long House, some 400 years old. Castle Farm is half a mile along George Lane at the west end of Marshfield, just north of the A420 Bristol(Kingswood) to Chippenham rd.

Bath

A city with a long history, much of which is visible today. Once the Roman town of Aquae Sulis, the site has been known to men much earlier than this, probably due to the finding by ancient man of the hot springs that come up from the ground. This is the only place in Britain where there is natural hot mineral springs gushing from the earth. Bath, the name we know it by today, is perhaps one of the oldest cities in the country, a great deal having been done to preserve not only its buildings but it's character as well. Many celebrities have lived or stayed in Bath at some time or other including Royal visitors, but the city owes as much to the three men, Beau Nash, Ralph Allen and John Wood as anyone. Beau Nash (real name Richard Nash) was a gambler from London and having won much money from people in Bath found a strong affection for the town. He brought Fashion and Society to Bath, which in turn brought money thus helping the city to prosper. With the help of Ralph Allen, postmaster and quarry owner many new and impressive buildings were erected to the designs of John Wood, technician and architect. The little picture above shows the Beckford Tower at Lansdown. At one time the private retreat of William Beckford, a wealthy man of many roles, but is now a museum to his memory. On the following page is a view of "Sham Castle", a folly built by Ralph Allen of Bath stone from his quarry. As a city, Bath is not big, and some

beautiful and interesting walks can be enjoyed in a short distance. There is every amenity here for the visitor no matter what their liking — museums, galleries and exhibitions for those who want to know, shops and restaurants, wonderful gardens to sit in and soak up the sun and sports of all kinds for the energetic ones. A major attraction of course, is the famous Roman Baths near the Abbey. The drawing on the right shows a modern structure marking the spot in what is called the King's Bath, where the hot spring comes up from the ground below. Bath, at the junction of the A4 and A46 close to Bristol and the M4/M5, is a must for everyone visiting the South Cotswolds.

INDEX

Acton Turville	27	Kingswood	11
Amberley	16		
		Lechlade	15
Badminton	27		
Bath	29, 30		
Berkeley Castle	7	Malmesbury	22
Berkeley	7	Map	centre pages
		Minchinhampton	9
Castle Combe	24, 25		
Castle Farm	28	Nags Head	9
Chalford	8, 9	Nailsworth	7
Cheltenham Spa	5	North Nibley	10
Chipping Sodbury	26	Nympsfield	10
Cirencester	20, 21		
Coates	22		
Cricklade	14	Ozleworth	23
Daglingworth	12, 13	Painswick	5
Dodington House	27		
Duntisbourne Rouse	12		
Dursley	11	Rodborough	6
Dyrham Park	28		
		South Cerney	15
Fairford	18, 19	Stroud	6
		Tetbury	23
Hawkesbury Upton	25	Thames Head	15
Hetty Peglers Tump	10		
		Westonbirt	26
Index	31	Wotton under Edge	14

THE TEN COMMANDMENTS - COUNTRY STYLE

The code is a set of ten reminders based on common sense — and common failings. So when in the country please remember:

    Guard against all risk of fire
    Fasten all gates
    Keep dogs under proper control
    Keep to the paths across farmland
    Avoid damaging fences, hedges and walls
    Leave no litter
    Safeguard water supplies
    Protect wildlife, wild plants and trees
    Go carefully on country roads
    Respect the life of the countryside
                    Thank you

Look out for our other productions -
    LOCAL PRINTS — POSTCARDS — PICTURES
    CALENDARS — CHRISTMAS CARDS
    WALKABOUT AND DRIVEABOUT GUIDES

Reardon & Son, Publishers

56 Upper Norwood Street, Leckhampton,
Cheltenham, Glos. GL53 0DU

Phone 231800 (STD 0242)

Whilst every care has been taken to ensure the accuracy of the information contained in this little book, neither the author or the publishers hold themselves responsible for any errors that may be found, or for a reader's interpretation of the text or illustrations.